KILLER COCKTAILS

MURDEROUSLY DELICIOUS LIBATIONS
INSPIRED BY HISTORY'S
MOST NOTORIOUS KILLERS

THE CONTROVERSIAL COCKTAIL CLUB
VOLUME 1

THORA POE PIERCE &
THORNE PHOBOS PAYNE

about us

Be introduced to the two wild and wonderful connoisseurs who are taking the world by storm.

They love a good tipple, a catchy tune, and a tall tale - but they're not too snooty about it. Along with their discerning taste, they're not afraid to get a little rowdy. In fact, they relish the seedier side of life, just for the fun of it. And let's not forget their feline muse, the one and only Gen. Pussy Talemonger - what a name, what a cat!

Together, they have embarked on a creative journey to write a series of books that are completely random, yet linked by their irreverent humour and general disregard for propriety. They don't care about respectability or purpose - they just want to make you laugh. They've got opinions, they've got humour, and they've got a disregard for the opinions of others - especially their friends. So don't take them too seriously, and don't take yourself too seriously either...just buckle up for a wild ride.

Come and join them on this journey of whimsy and wonder, where the joy of life is celebrated with every page.

The Controversial Cocktail Club

Welcome, dear reader, to a series of cocktail books like no other – a concoction of murderously delicious libations inspired by history's most notorious killers, both real and imagined. But before you dive into this macabre mixology, be warned: this tome is steeped in tongue-in-cheek humour and not to be taken too seriously. After all, we're here to explore the dark side of history and literature with a cocktail shaker in hand, not a dagger!

So, as you turn these pages, remember: all visuals are purely for illustration purposes. We're stirring up history with a swizzle stick, not a scalpel. Don't expect a true crime exposé or a somber historical tome. Instead, prepare for a whimsical whirlwind tour through a landscape where cocktails are named after infamous characters, and the only thing we're killing is time.

Buckle up for a wild ride through a world where whimsy reigns supreme, and the joy of living is toasted with every sip. Whether you're here for the tales or the cocktails, you're in for a treat. Let the revelry begin, and remember: it's all in good spirits.

Gin

London Fog	10
Clinical Cleanse	12
Clinical Spirits	14
Victorian Secrets	16
Seaside Remedy	18
Post-War Brew	20
Jazz Age Fizz	22

Vodka

Bathhouse Elixir	26
Iron Maiden	28
Soapy Elixir	30
Hospital Hush	32
Red Lipstick Martini	34

Bourbon, Whisky, Whiskey

Ironclad	38
Blackout Old Fashioned	40
Boston Fog	42
Highland Mist	44
Dusty Cellar	46
Farmland Folly	48
Southern Comfort	50
Nomadic Smoke	52
Diner's Deceit	54
Chicago Smoke	56
Lonely Lens	58
Arsenic Dollar	60
Bloody Butcher	62
Homely Poison	64

Wine, Vermouth, Sherry

Sweet Deception	68
Poisoned Chalice	70
Noble Poison	72
Countryside Blood	74

Rum

Hippie Trail	78
Acidic Cologne	80
Sailor's Delight	82
Salty Brig	84
Acidic Cologne	86
Flint's Loot	88

Tequila & Liqueur

Dusty Road	92
Castle's Echo	94
Mexico City Nights	96
Acid Trip	98
Black Forest Brew	100
German Hearth	102

Brandy & Cognac

Medieval Majesty	106
Parisian Deceit	108
Parisian Close Quarters	110
Rustic Italian	112

Other

GIN

In the shadowy, mist-filled streets of Victorian London,
Jack the Ripper lurked, his presence leaving behind
a chilling blend of damp cobblestone and an air of terror,
as thick and enigmatic as the London fog itself.

London Fog

Ingredients

2 oz Gin
1 oz Earl Grey tea syrup
0.5 oz fresh lemon juice
Soda water

Recipe

Mix gin, Earl Grey syrup, and lemon juice in a shaker with ice.
Shake well and strain into a glass.
Top with soda water.

Step into the eerie mist of Victorian London with a
cocktail shrouded in mystery and as hauntingly
complex as the unsolved riddles of the infamous
Whitechapel murders."

'Richard Speck's heinous act in a Chicago townhouse left an indelible mark, the air tainted with the clinical, antiseptic scent of a nurse's dormitory, underlain with the palpable terror of his brutal rampage.

CLINICAL CLEANSE

Ingredients

2 oz Gin
1 oz White grape juice
0.5 oz Lime juice
Mint sprig

Recipe

Shake gin, grape juice, and lime juice with ice.
Strain into a chilled glass and garnish with a mint sprig.

Sterilise your palate with a concoction as cold
and clinical as Speck's own calculated brutality.

In the sterile corridors of the hospital, Jane Toppan moved with a healer's grace, yet her touch left a trail as chilling and clinical as the antiseptic air, masking her deadly cravings beneath a veneer of care.

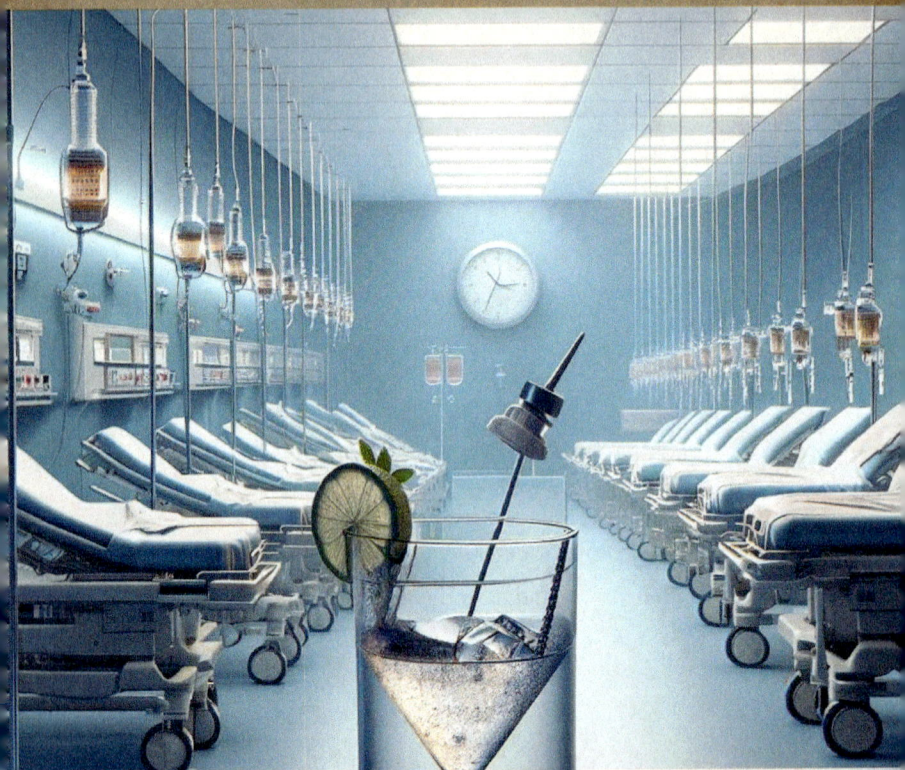

Clinical Spirits

Ingredients

2 oz Gin

0.5 oz Dry Vermouth

0.5 oz Elderflower Liqueur

0.5 oz Fresh Lemon Juice

2 dashes of Peppermint Bitters

Club Soda (to top off)

Lemon twist or a sprig of fresh mint for garnish

Recipe

In a mixing glass, combine the gin, dry vermouth, elderflower liqueur, and fresh lemon juice.

Add the peppermint bitters.

Fill the mixing glass with ice and stir the mixture gently.

Strain the mixture into a highball glass filled with ice.

Top the cocktail with a splash of club soda.

Garnish with a lemon twist or a sprig of fresh mint.

Experience a deceptively soothing blend that conceals a dangerous edge, much like the angel of death herself.

In the quiet domesticity of Victorian England,
Mary Ann Cotton's presence was as comforting
as a warm cup of tea, yet laced with a sinister undercurrent,
a whisper of arsenic subtly tainting her genteel facade.

Victorian Secret

Ingredients

2 oz Earl Grey tea-infused Gin
1 oz Lemon juice
0.5 oz Simple syrup
Lemon twist

Recipe

Infuse gin with Earl Grey tea.
Then mix with lemon juice and syrup in a shaker with ice.
Strain into a chilled glass and garnish with a lemon twist.

Indulge in the dark romance of Victorian England
with a drink as deadly and deceptive as the
arsenic-laced tea of Mary Ann Cotton.

Dr. John Bodkin Adams left an enigmatic scent in his wake, a blend of seaside air and medicinal herbs that wafted through the corridors of Eastbourne, as mysterious and elusive as the doctor himself.

SEASIDE REMEDY

Ingredients

2 oz Gin
1 oz Sea salt solution (brine)
0.5 oz Elderflower liqueur
0.5 oz Lime juice

Recipe

Shake gin, brine, elderflower liqueur, and lime juice with ice.
Strain into a chilled glass.

INHALE THE BRACING SEA AIR OF EASTBOURNE
WITH A MEDICINAL COCKTAIL AS INTRIGUING
AS THE DOCTOR'S OWN AMBIGUOUS LEGACY.

In post-war England, Mary Elizabeth Wilson's presence was marked by a disturbing contrast, the comforting scent of tea hiding the deadly trace of antifreeze, as deceptive as her outwardly normal appearance.

POST-WAR BREW

Ingredients

2 oz Gin
1 oz Earl Grey tea
0.5 oz Lemon juice
Dash of tonic water.

Recipe

Brew Earl Grey tea and let it cool.
Shake gin, tea, and lemon juice with ice.
Strain into a glass and top with tonic water.

**SIP ON THE AUSTERITY AND HIDDEN DANGERS
OF POST-WAR ENGLAND, ENCAPSULATED IN A
COCKTAIL AS UNASSUMING AND LETHAL
AS WILSON'S METHODS.**

Amidst the roaring twenties in America, Ruth Snyder moved with a certain flair, her life filled with the scents of jazz-era perfume and gin, masking the turmoil and betrayal behind her glamorous facade.

Jazz Age Fizz

Ingredients

2 oz Gin
1 oz Lemon juice
0.5 oz Simple syrup
Champagne to top
Lemon twist for garnish

Recipe

Shake gin, lemon juice, and syrup with ice.
Strain into a glass and top with Champagne.
Garnish with a lemon twist.

REVEL IN THE ROARING TWENTIES WITH A DRINK AS BOLD
AND REBELLIOUS AS SNYDER'S INFAMOUS ESCAPADE.

Vodka

In the quiet domesticity of early 20th-century England, George Joseph Smith cast a shadow over the serene bathhouses, where the seemingly tranquil water masked his sinister deeds, leaving an air of chlorinated suspicion in his wake.

Bathhouse Elixir

Ingredients

2 oz Vodka
1 oz Blue Curacao
1 oz Lemon juice
Soda water

Recipe

Combine vodka, Blue Curacao, and lemon juice in a shaker with ice.
Shake well and strain into a glass filled with ice.
Top with soda water.

Plunge into the deceptive tranquillity of Smith's world,
where danger lurks beneath the surface of a
seemingly serene drink.

The streets of Düsseldorf were haunted by the presence of Peter Kürten, the 'Vampire of Düsseldorf,' his deeds leaving a metallic tang of blood in the air, a scent as chilling as his unpredictable violence.

Iron Maiden

Ingredients

2 oz Vodka
1 oz Tomato juice
0.5 oz Lemon juice
Pinch of salt
Worcestershire sauce

Recipe

Combine ingredients in a shaker with ice.
Shake and strain into a chilled glass.
Add a dash of Worcestershire sauce.

Unleash the chilling thrill of the hunt
with a cocktail that's as dark and enigmatic
as the Vampire of Düsseldorf.

The hallways of a hospital carried the troubling essence of Genene Jones, a mix of sterile, clinical air and an underlying sense of dread, cloaking her sinister activities in a place of healing.

Hospital Hush

Ingredients

2 oz Vodka
1 oz White cranberry juice
0.5 oz Lime juice
Splash of soda water.

Recipe

Shake vodka, cranberry juice, and lime juice with ice.
Strain into a chilled glass and top with soda water.

Delve into the deceptive calm of a hospital with a cocktail that masks its sinister undertones as effectively as Jones concealed her crimes.

In the seemingly quaint town of Correggio, Leonarda Cianciulli's home held a macabre secret, the air tainted with the caustic aroma of lye, masking the gruesome reality of her ghastly deeds.

Correggio's Secret

Ingredients

2 oz Vodka
1 oz Lavender syrup
0.5 oz Lemon juice
Lavender sprig for garnish

Recipe

Shake vodka, lavender syrup, and lemon juice with ice.
Strain into a chilled glass and garnish with a lavender sprig.

Cleanse your palate with a concoction as unsettling and bizarre
as the Soap-Maker of Correggio's gruesome tale

The city of Chicago felt the lurking presence
of William 'Heirens, the 'Lipstick 'Killer,'
his trail marked by a bold, waxy scent of lipstick,
as haunting and indelible as the messages he left behind.

Red Lipstick Martini

Ingredients

2 oz Vodka
1 oz Cranberry juice
0.5 oz Triple sec
Lime wedge

Recipe

Shake vodka, cranberry juice, triple sec with ice.
Strain into a martini glass.
Garnish with a lime wedge.

Savour a drink that's as bold and enigmatic
as the messages left by the Lipstick Killer,
with a twist of mystery in every sip.

Bourbon,
whisky,
whiskey

The transient life of Jake Bird, a wandering axe murderer, was marked by the metallic tang of his weapon and the earthy scent of the open road, as he drifted through the United States leaving a trail of violence.

Ironclad

Ingredients

2 oz Scotch Whisky
1 oz Drambuie
Lemon twist

Recipe

Pour whisky and Drambuie into a glass with ice.
Stir well and garnish with a lemon twist.

Taste the steely resolve of a drifter's journey,
encapsulated in a cocktail as robust and enduring
as Bird's own tale.

During the blackouts of WWII London, Gordon Cummins, the 'Blackout Ripper,' prowled the streets, his presence as dark and menacing as the smog-filled air, a sinister figure shrouded in the city's wartime fear and shadows.

BLACKOUT OLD FASHIONED

Ingredients

2 oz Smoked Whiskey
1 sugar cube
2 dashes Angostura bitters
Orange peel

Recipe

Muddle the sugar cube and bitters in a glass.
Add whiskey and ice, and stir.
Garnish with a flamed orange peel for smoky aroma.

Brave the darkened streets of wartime London with a cocktail that's as mysterious and potent as the Blackout Ripper's legacy.

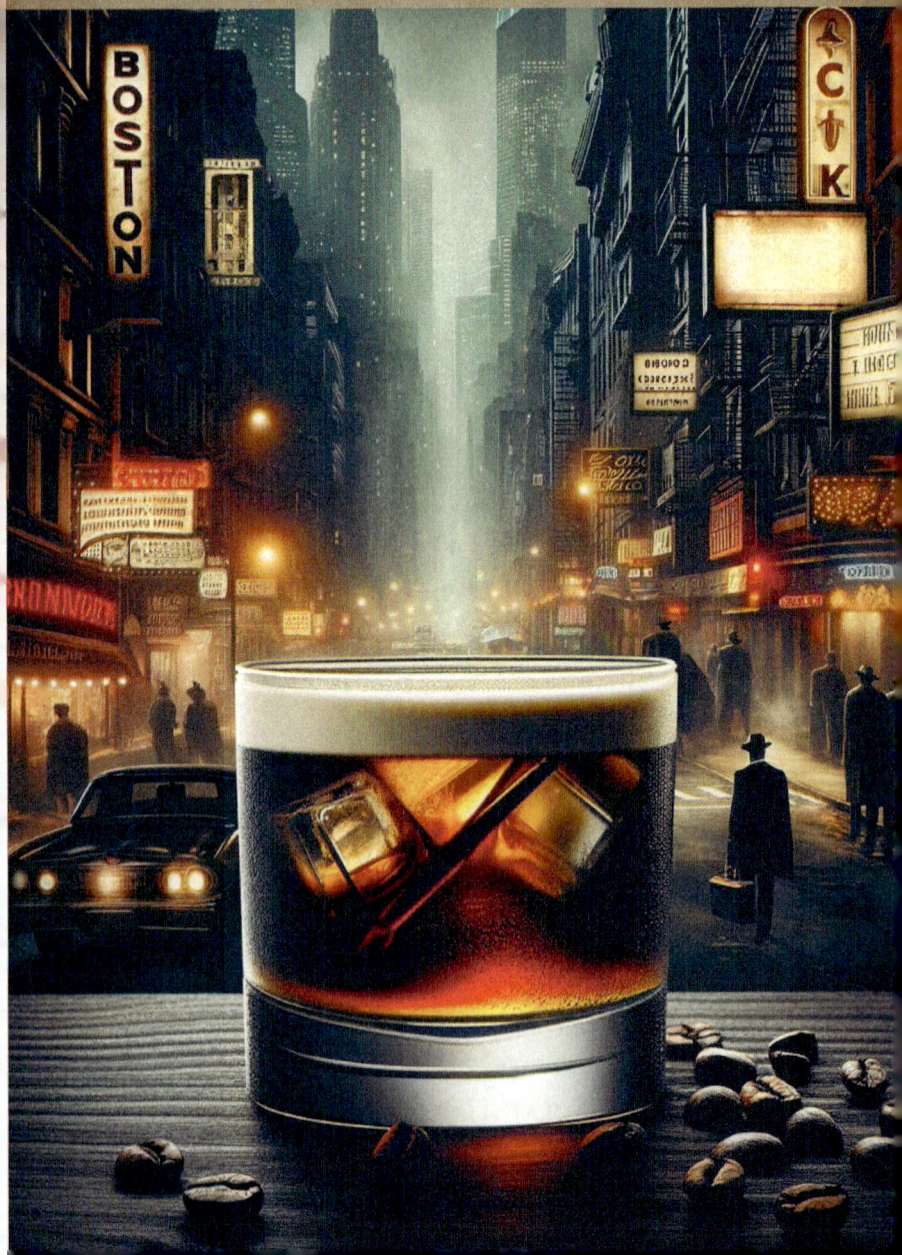

In the changing landscape of 1960s Boston, Albert DeSalvo, known as the 'Boston Strangler,' moved undetected, his presence blending into the urban backdrop, leaving behind an unsettling mix of city grime and the hidden terror of his crimes.

BOSTON FOG

Ingredients

2 oz Irish Whiskey
1 oz Coffee Liqueur
1 oz Cream
Dash of cinnamon

Recipe

Shake whiskey, coffee liqueur, and cream with ice.
Strain into an old-fashioned glass and sprinkle with cinnamon.

Navigate the complex layers of 60s Boston, with a cocktail both enigmatic and controversial as the Boston Strangler himself.

The Scottish-American Peter Manuel brought a cold, damp terror to the highlands, his acts as sinister as the wet earth and heather of his hunting grounds, leaving communities shrouded in a chilling, pervasive dread.

Highland Mist

Ingredients

2 oz Whisky
1 oz Đrambuie
0.5 oz Lemon juice
Đash of Peychaud's bitters

Recipe

Combine whisky, Đrambuie, lemon juice, and bitters in a shaker
with ice.
Shake and strain into a glass.

VENTURE INTO THE CHILLING DEPTHS OF THE SCOTTISH
HIGHLANDS WITH A DRINK THAT CAPTURES THE
HAUNTING ESSENCE OF MANUEL'S REIGN OF TERROR.

Within the eerie confines of his Chicago 'Murder Castle,' H.H. Holmes weaved a labyrinth of death, the air heavy with the musty scent of his concealed rooms, echoing with the muffled despair of his victims.

DUSTY CELLAR

Ingredients

2 oz Aged Bourbon
1 oz Amontillado Sherry
0.5 oz Bénédictine liqueur
2 dashes of Angostura bitters
Orange peel (for garnish)
A small pinch of edible gold dust (optional, for presentation)

Recipe

In a mixing glass, combine the aged bourbon, Amontillado sherry, and
Bénédictine liqueur.
Add the Angostura bitters.
Fill the mixing glass with ice and stir the ingredients until chilled.
Strain the cocktail into a chilled old-fashioned coupe glass.
Express the oils of an orange peel over the drink, garnish with the peel.
As an optional touch, sprinkle a small pinch of edible gold dust.

**Descend into shadowy depths of intrigue with a blend as
enigmatic and complex as Holmes' own twisted labyrinth.**

Amidst the rural farmlands of early 20th-century America, Belle Gunness lured her victims, her presence as nurturing and bountiful as the fertile soil, yet hiding a darkness as deep as the nearby livestock's restless murmurs.

Farmland Folly

Ingredients

2 oz Bourbon
1 oz Apple cider
0.5 oz Lemon juice
Dash of cinnamon

Recipe

Combine bourbon, cider, lemon juice, and cinnamon in a shaker
with ice.
Shake well and strain into a glass filled with ice.

Harvest the sinister secrets of the farmland with a cocktail
as robust and earthy as Gunness's rural reign of terror.

Nannie Doss, the 'Giggling Granny,' filled her Southern kitchen with the aroma of sweet, home-cooked meals, a deceptively cozy ambiance that masked the bitter poison of her intentions.

Southern Comfort

Ingredients

2 oz Bourbon
1 oz Peach nectar
0.5 oz Honey syrup
Dash of bitters

Recipe

Shake bourbon, peach nectar, honey syrup, and bitters with ice.
Strain into an old-fashioned glass with ice.

Savour the sweetness laced with hidden
danger, reminiscent of the Giggling Granny's
lethal home-cooked meals.

Drifting across America, Earle Nelson's path was as elusive as smoke, his transient nature leaving a trail tinged with the scent of train smoke and the worn leather of his well-travelled boots.

NOMADIC SMOKE

Ingredients

2 oz Smoked Whiskey
1 oz Sweet Vermouth
2 dashes Orange bitters
Orange peel

Recipe

Stir whiskey, vermouth, and bitters with ice.
Strain into a chilled glass and garnish with an orange peel.

DRIFT THROUGH THE GRITTY UNDERCURRENTS
OF AMERICA WITH A SMOKY COCKTAIL AS TRANSIENT
AND ELUSIVE AS THE GORILLA KILLER HIMSELF.

In the American South of the 1930s to 1950s, Rhonda Belle Martin's home was a place of deceptive hospitality, where the comforting smell of coffee and home cooking hid a dangerous, toxic undercurrent.

DINER'S DECEIT

Ingredients

2 oz Coffee-infused Bourbon
1 oz Cream
0.5 oz Maple syrup
Dash of vanilla extract

Recipe

Infuse bourbon with coffee.
Shake the infused bourbon, cream, maple syrup, and vanilla with ice.
Strain into a glass.

SIT DOWN TO A COMFORTING YET DECEPTIVE BLEND,
ECHOING THE TREACHEROUS HOSPITALITY OF MARTIN'S DINER.

The streets near the Hanover train station bore the unseen mark of Fritz Haarmann, where the unsettling scent of raw meat from his butcher shop mingled with an underlying, sinister foreboding.

Bloody Butcher

Ingredients

2 oz Rye Whiskey
1 oz Beet juice
0.5 oz Lemon juice
0.5 oz Honey syrup

Recipe

Shake all ingredients with ice.
Strain into a chilled glass.

Dare to taste the darker side of history
with a concoction that's as hauntingly bold
as Haarmann's shadowy legacy.

In the heart of early 20th-century Chicago, Tillie Klimek's presence was felt like a dense fog of industrial smoke, intermingled with the comforting, yet deceiving aroma of her home-cooked meals, masking the darker intentions beneath.

Chicago Smoke

Ingredients

2 oz Rye Whiskey
1 oz Sweet Vermouth
2 dashes of liquid smoke
Cherry for garnish

Recipe

Stir whiskey, vermouth, and liquid smoke with ice.
Strain into a chilled glass and garnish with a cherry.

Immerse yourself in the gritty spirit of the Windy
City, with a cocktail as dark and smoky as
Klimek's urban legend.

Amidst the loneliness of mid-20th-century American cities, Harvey Glatman lurked, his presence marked by the faint, haunting aroma of old camera film, capturing more than just images in his chilling pursuit.

Lonely Lens

Ingredients

2 oz Bourbon
1 oz Coffee liqueur
Dash of bitters
Coffee bean for garnish

Recipe

Stir bourbon, coffee liqueur, and bitters over ice.
Strain into an old-fashioned glass and garnish with a coffee bean.

Capture the solitude of the city
with a reflective drink as introspective
and haunting as Glatman's lonely crimes.

Johann Otto Hoch walked the early 20th-century American landscape with a deceptive air, his presence infused with the smell of money and a hidden trace of arsenic, as elusive as his many aliases.

Arsenic Dollar

Ingredients

2 oz Rye Whiskey
1 oz Apple cider
0.5 oz Maple syrup
Dash of aromatic bitters

Recipe

Shake whiskey, cider, syrup, and bitters with ice.
Strain into an old-fashioned glass with ice.

Taste the greed and deception of early America in a
cocktail as intoxicating and dangerous as Hoch's
poisonous ventures.

In the seemingly comforting American homes, Anna Marie 'Hahn's presence was as warm and inviting as home-cooked meals, yet laced with a toxic, deceptive undertone that belied her true nature.

Homely Poison

Ingredients

2 oz Bourbon
1 oz Apple cider
0.5 oz Cinnamon syrup
Apple slice for garnish

Recipe

Shake bourbon, cider, and cinnamon syrup with ice.
Strain into an ice-filled glass and garnish with an apple slice.

Cosy up with a drink that's as comforting and
treacherous as the deceptively lethal meals prepared
by the Poisoning Widow.

Wine, vermouth and sherry

The deceptive duo, Martha Beck and Raymond Fernandez, spun a web of romantic deceit, their trail marked by the cheap, sweet scent of perfume and cologne, cloaking the danger of their 'Lonely Hearts' escapades.

Sweet Deception

Ingredients

2 oz Rosé wine
1 oz Elderflower liqueur
0.5 oz Lemon juice
Splash of grenadine

Recipe

Mix rosé, elderflower liqueur, and lemon juice in a shaker with ice.
Strain into a glass and add a splash of grenadine.

Get swept away by a romance laced with danger, in a drink that's as tantalisingly sweet as their twisted tales.

Vera Renczi's boudoir was a place of seductive secrets, the air
rich with the intoxicating aroma of fine wine, each glass
concealing a metallic hint of the poison that was her trademark.

POISONED CHALICE

Ingredients

2 oz Red Wine
1 oz Brandy
0.5 oz Blackberry liqueur
Blackberries for garnish

Recipe

Pour wine, brandy, and liqueur into a glass with ice.
Stir gently and garnish with blackberries.

TEMPT FATE WITH A BEGUILING MIX THAT'S AS
SEDUCTIVE AND DANGEROUS AS THE BLACK
WIDOW'S VENOMOUS CHARM

Madame de Brinvilliers, a figure of aristocratic decadence in 17th-century France, moved through the corridors of intrigue, her path scented with the intoxicating blend of perfume and the subtle, lethal hint of poison.

Noble Poison

Ingredients

2 oz Champagne
1 oz Elderflower liqueur
0.5 oz Absinthe
Lemon twist for garnish

Recipe

Pour elderflower liqueur and absinthe into a champagne flute.
Top with champagne and garnish with a lemon twist.

Indulge in the lavish decadence
of French nobility, with a cocktail as rich
and lethal as the aristocrat's deadly potions.

Roaming the French countryside, Joseph Vacher brought a scent of fields and blood, a pastoral nightmare that unfolded under the open sky, as unpredictable and terrifying as the 'French Ripper' himself.

Countryside Blood

Ingredients

2 oz Red Wine
1 oz Brandy
0.5 oz Blackberry liqueur
Berry for garnish

Recipe

Pour wine, brandy, and blackberry liqueur into a glass with ice.
Stir gently and garnish with a berry.

Traverse the French countryside with a drink as rustic
and blood-tinted as the footprint of the French Ripper.

Rum

The 'Bikini Killer,' Charles Sobhraj, haunted the exotic routes of Asia, his crimes leaving behind a trail of spicy, incense-laden air, as intoxicating and dangerous as his charm and deceit.

HIPPIE TRAIL

Ingredients

2 oz Spiced Rum
1 oz Mango juice
0.5 oz Lime juice
Dash of cinnamon

Recipe

Shake rum, mango juice, lime juice, and cinnamon with ice.
Strain into an ice-filled glass.

Embark on an exotic journey down the Hippie Trail
with a blend as spicy and deceptive as Sobhraj's
infamous escapades.

Aboard the USS Caine, Captain Queeg's authority filled the air, as tense and rigid as the metallic tang of naval machinery, mixed with the saltiness of the sea, a reflection of his paranoid command and the crew's mounting tension.

The Caine's Edge

Ingredients

2 oz Navy Strength Rum

0.5 oz Lime Juice

0.5 oz Ginger Syrup

2 dashes of Angostura Bitters

A small scoop of crushed ice

Lime wheel for garnish

Optional: A small edible maraschino cherry

Recipe

In a shaker, combine the rum, lime juice, and ginger syrup.

Add the Angostura bitters.

Fill the shaker with ice and shake vigorously.

Strain the mixture into a glass filled with crushed ice.

Garnish with a lime wheel and, if desired, a maraschino cherry.

Step into the tense and tumultuous world where strict discipline and growing paranoia steer a course through stormy psychological seas.

Frederick Bailey Ðeeming sailed the seas, his essence as vast and unfathomable as the ocean, the saltwater and ship wood scenting his journey with the brine of adventure and the shadow of his hidden horrors.

SAILOR'S DELIGHT

Ingredients

2 oz Dark Rum
1 oz Pineapple juice
0.5 oz Coconut cream
Dash of nutmeg

Recipe

Shake rum, pineapple juice, and coconut cream with ice.
Strain into an ice-filled glass and sprinkle with nutmeg.

SET SAIL ON A JOURNEY OF MYSTERY WITH A
MARITIME COCKTAIL AS ENIGMATIC AS DEEMING'S OWN
TWISTED TRAVELS.

Through the cold, harsh prisons and across the sea on stolen ships, Carl Panzram roamed, his path marked by an air of defiance, as cold and unyielding as the metal and saltwater that defined his turbulent life.

SALTY BRIG

Ingredients

2 oz Dark Rum
0.5 oz Lime juice
0.5 oz Simple syrup
Pinch of sea salt

Recipe

Shake rum, lime juice, syrup, and salt with ice.
Strain into an ice-filled glass.

Navigate the rough seas of a rebel's soul with
a cocktail that's as brash and unapologetic as
Panzram's own storied life.

'In post-war England, John George Haigh, the 'Acid Bath Murderer,' conducted his ghastly affairs behind a veneer of respectability, the chemical odour of his gruesome method belying the facade of his outward charm.

Acidic Cologne

Ingredients

2 oz Aged Rum
1 oz Pineapple juice
0.5 oz Lime juice
0.5 oz Simple syrup
Splash of bitters

Recipe

Combine all ingredients in a shaker with ice.
Shake and strain into a glass.
Add a splash of bitters.

Dive into a complex mix of flavours that's as smooth
and deceptive as the Acid Bath Murderer's
outward charm.

Though unseen, the legend of Captain Flint haunted every pirate's tale, his presence as elusive as a wisp of sea air, carrying the promise of treasure and adventure, the scent of the ocean mingling with the mystery of his untold stories.

FLiNT's LooT

Ingredients

2 oz Dark Rum

0.5 oz Smoky Scotch Whisky

0.5 oz Amaretto

1 oz Fresh lime juice

0.5 oz Simple syrup

A dash of Angostura bitters

Ice cubes

Lime wheel for garnish

Optional: A small piece of edible gold leaf or gold dust

Recipe

In a cocktail shaker, pour the rum, whisky, amaretto, fresh lime juice, simple syrup, and a dash of Angostura bitters.
Fill the shaker with ice and shake vigorously.
Strain the mixture into a rocks glass filled with ice cubes.
Garnish with a lime wheel, or float a small piece of edible gold leaf.

Cruise the treacherous waters of pirate lore, capturing the smoky mystery and hidden riches of the legendary buccaneer's untold tales.

Tequila and Liqueur

Drifting across the American landscape, Carroll Cole's path was marked by the dusty roads and transient nature of his existence, his crimes leaving an imprint as fleeting and elusive as the many towns he passed through.

Dusty Road

Ingredients

2 oz Mezcal
1 oz Fresh lime juice
0.5 oz Agave nectar (or simple syrup)
0.5 oz Cointreau or Triple Sec
A pinch of smoked sea salt
Crushed ice
Lime wheel and a sprig of thyme for garnish
Optional: a small dash of chilli powder for an extra kick

Recipe

In a shaker, combine mezcal, fresh lime, agave nectar, and Cointreau.
Add a pinch of smoked sea salt and a small dash of chilli powder.
Fill the shaker with ice and shake vigorously until well-chilled.
Strain the mixture into a glass filled with crushed ice.
Garnish with a lime wheel and a sprig of thyme.

Hit the open road with a cocktail that's as rugged and restless as Cole's cross-country crimes.

The chambers of Elizabeth Báthory were as chilling and sterile as her heart, the cold stone and iron of her castle echoing the bloodlust that stained her legacy.

CASTLE'S ECHO

Ingredients

2 oz Silver Tequila
1 oz Lime juice
0.5 oz Agave syrup
Salt for rimming

Recipe

Rim a glass with salt.
Shake tequila, lime juice, and agave syrup with ice.
Strain into the prepared glass.

STEP INTO THE CHILLING CORRIDORS OF HISTORY WITH A DRINK AS COLD
AND ENIGMATIC AS THE BLOOD COUNTESS HERSELF.

The vibrant streets of early 20th-century Mexico City echoed with the steps of Francisco Guerrero Pérez, his passage leaving a trail of danger amidst the enticing aromas of street food, as unpredictable as the 'Mexican Jack the Ripper.'

MEXICO CITY NIGHTS

Ingredients

2 oz Tequila
1 oz Lime juice
0.5 oz Agave syrup
Dash of hot sauce

Recipe

Shake tequila, lime juice, agave syrup, and hot sauce with ice.
Strain into a chilled glass.

Immerse yourself in the vibrant yet perilous streets
of early 20th-century Mexico City with a cocktail as
lively and risky as Guerrero Pérez's legacy.

John 'Haigh, the 'Acid Bath Murderer,' prowled post-war England, his crimes veiled behind a façade of charm, leaving behind an acidic, chemical trace as pungent and shocking as his method of disposal.

Acid Trip

Ingredients

2 oz Tequila
1 oz Lime juice
0.5 oz Agave syrup
1 Egg white

Recipe

Dry shake all ingredients without ice, then add ice and shake again.
Strain into a glass.

Experience a cocktail with a bite, blending sharp flavours
for a sensation as startling as Naigh's infamous method.

Whispered tales circled Peter Stumpp, the 'Werewolf of Bedburg,' whose presence was as earthy and primal as the deep, dark woods of 16th-century Germany, a hint of pine mingling with the unsettling sense of lurking danger.

Black Forest Brew

Ingredients

2 oz Jägermeister
1 oz Blackberry liqueur
0.5 oz Lemon juice
Sprig of pine for garnish

Recipe

Shake Jägermeister, blackberry liqueur, and lemon juice with ice.
Strain into a chilled glass and garnish with a pine sprig.

Venture into the shadowy depths of German folklore
with a concoction as dark and mysterious as the
Werewolf of Bedburg.

In the quiet isolation of early 20th-century German towns, Fritz Angerstein moved like a shadow, his presence as cold and hard as coal and wood, an ominous figure haunting the sleepy streets.

German Hearth

Ingredients

2 oz Jägermeister
1 oz Dark beer
0.5 oz Lemon juice
Dash of cinnamon

Recipe

Combine Jägermeister, beer, and lemon juice in a glass with ice.
Stir gently and sprinkle with cinnamon.

Warm up with a hearty cocktail that echoes the isolation and smoky undertones of early 20th-century German towns.

Brandy and Cognac

In the grandeur of mediaeval France, Gilles de Rais was a figure of opulence and decay, the air around him thick with the heavy scent of incense and the cold, unyielding aroma of ancient stone.

Medieval Majesty

Ingredients

2 oz Brandy
1 oz Red wine
0.5 oz Simple syrup
Dash of aromatic bitters

Recipe

Combine brandy, wine, syrup, and bitters in a mixing glass with ice.
Stir well and strain into a wine glass.

Embark on a journey back in time with a drink as
opulent and sinister as the dark legacy of de Rais.

In the charming streets of early 20th-century Paris,
Henri Désiré Landru exuded a deceptive allure,
his sophisticated air infused with the rich scent of tobacco
and fine wine, veiling his sinister pursuits.

PARISIAN DECEIT

Ingredients

2 oz Cognac
1 oz Red wine
0.5 oz Cointreau
Orange peel for garnish

Recipe

Combine cognac, wine, and Cointreau in a mixing glass with ice.
Stir well and strain into a wine glass.
Garnish with orange peel.

INDULGE IN THE DECEPTIVE ALLURE OF EARLY
20TH-CENTURY PARIS WITH A DRINK AS SMOOTH
AND DANGEROUS AS BLUEBEARD'S CHARM.

Within the close quarters of early 20th-century Parisian apartments, Jeanne Weber's figure loomed, the air heavy with the mustiness of cramped spaces, echoing the suffocating dread of her heinous acts.

Parisian Close Quarters

Ingredients

2 oz French Brandy
1 oz Amaretto
0.5 oz Lemon juice
Dash of bitters

Recipe

Shake brandy, amaretto, lemon juice, and bitters with ice.
Strain into a chilled glass.

Squeeze into the dense atmosphere of a Parisian
apartment with a drink as complex and
suffocating as Weber's twisted mind.

In the rustic Italian countryside of the early 20th century, the air around Giuseppe Greco was tinged with the fresh scent of earth and olives, a pastoral tranquility that belied the violence of his actions.

Rustic Italian

Ingredients

2 oz Grappa
1 oz Olive juice
0.5 oz Lemon juice
Olive for garnish

Recipe

Shake grappa, olive juice, and lemon juice with ice.
Strain into a chilled glass and garnish with an olive.

Stroll through the rustic Italian countryside with a
drink as earthy and robust as Greco's rural reign.

Other

Amidst the genteel society of early 20th-century Belgium, Marie Becker's refined presence was tainted with a hidden danger, the scent of fine tea mingling with a subtle, poisonous undercurrent.

Belgian Elegance

Ingredients

2 oz Genever
1 oz Chamomile tea
0.5 oz Honey syrup
Lemon twist for garnish

Recipe

Brew chamomile tea and let it cool.
Shake genever, tea, and syrup with ice.
Strain into a chilled glass and garnish with a lemon twist.

Experience the genteel charm of early 20th-century Belgium, with a sophisticated drink masking a dangerous undercurrent.

In the desolate outskirts of Tehran,
the 'Tehran Desert Vampire', Mohammed Bijeh, lurked,
his presence as haunting and barren as the desert itself,
charged with an air of fear and desolation.

Desert Mirage

Ingredients

2 oz Arak
1 oz Pomegranate juice
0.5 oz Lime juice
Splash of rose water

Recipe

Shake arak, pomegranate juice, lime juice, and rose water with ice.
Strain into a chilled glass.

Wander the desolate outskirts of Tehran with a
drink that reflects the harshness and fear of the
Desert Vampire's domain.

Across the remote and rugged landscape of the Andes,
Luis Gregorio Ramírez Maestre cast a shadow of desperation,
the mountain air carrying the weight of his dark deeds.

ANDEAN BREATH

Ingredients

2 oz Pisco

1 oz Chicha Morada (Peruvian purple corn drink)

0.5 oz Lime juice

Dash of bitters.

Recipe

Shake pisco, chicha morada, lime juice, and bitters with ice.
Strain into a glass filled with ice.

SCALE THE HEIGHTS OF THE ANDES
WITH A COCKTAIL AS FRESH AND DESPERATE
AS THE AIR IN RAMÍREZ MAESTRE'S
MOUNTAINOUS HAUNTS.

In the dank, narrow streets of 19th-century Edinburgh, Burke and Hare's sinister trade cast a grim shadow, their deeds marked by the musty scent of wet stone and old ale, a macabre undercurrent beneath the city's bustling surface.

EDINBURGH DRAUGHT

Ingredients

2 oz Scotch Ale
1 oz Scotch Whisky
0.5 oz Honey syrup
Lemon twist.

Recipe

Combine Scotch ale, whisky, and honey syrup in a glass with ice.
Stir gently and garnish with a lemon twist.

UNCOVER THE DARK UNDERBELLY OF EDINBURGH WITH A DRINK THAT'S
AS RICH IN HISTORY AS BURKE AND HARE'S NOTORIOUS DEEDS.

Neville Heath, a charmer turned killer, brought a sense of danger to post-war Britain, his deeds leaving a lingering scent of leather and ale from the pubs where his deceptive allure found its victims.

Leather & Ale

Ingredients

2 oz Brown Ale
1 oz Bourbon
0.5 oz Maple syrup
Dash of bitters

Recipe

Combine bourbon, maple syrup, and bitters in a glass.
Top with brown ale and stir gently.

*Immerse yourself in the post-war glamour with a drink
that's as charming and dangerous as Heath's own
deceptive allure.*

The Controversial Cocktail Club

continues in Volume 2

Your cocktail notes

Printed in Great Britain
by Amazon